Basic Tools for College Composition Success

For Beginner Students in ESL 0090

By

Gina Vellani

Revised Fall 2023

innovativeink
PUBLISHING

www.innovativeinkpublishing.com
Send all inquiries to:
4050 Westmark Drive
Dubuque, IA 52004-1840

ISBN: 979-8-3851-5223-0

Published in the United States of America

Table of Contents

Dedicated to all the amazing students in my Spring 2019 and Spring 2020 ESL 0100 classes. Thank you so much for sharing your essays to make this resource more authentic. I am looking forward to seeing you walk across the platform at graduation someday soon! – Gina Vellani

Chapter 1: Paragraph Writing Basics

What is a paragraph?

A paragraph is 3 or more sentences about one topic or idea.

A paragraph has 3 main parts:

1. Topic sentence: The first sentence. It has the main idea of the paragraph.
2. Supporting sentences: The middle sentences. They give information about the topic.
3. Concluding sentence: The last sentence. It repeats the main idea of the paragraph or gives the writer's personal opinion.

"Fish sandwich" by Kim Siever is marked with Public Domain Mark 1.0. https://creativecommons.org/publicdomain/mark/1.0/?ref=openverse.

A good paragraph is like a sandwich. The topic sentence and the concluding sentence is the bread, and the supporting sentences are the ingredients inside: meat, cheese, and lettuce.

EXAMPLE PARAGRAPH # 1

A Good Teacher

Good teachers have many important qualities. They are patient. When students do not understand, they explain information again. They are very organized. Good teachers prepare for every class. Students can learn easily with an organized teacher. Good teachers are also caring. They help students and listen to students with problems. Finally, good teachers are fair. They do not give too much homework and they give impartial grades. My English teacher has every quality of a good teacher.

"students-in-class-with-teacher-reading" by www.ilmicrofono. https://creativecommons.org/licenses/by/2.0/?ref=openverse.

<u>Activity 1</u>

Underline the topic sentence.

1. What are the qualities of a good teacher? ____________________________

____

2. Underline the concluding sentence.
3. Do you like this paragraph? Why? Why not? ____________________________

____

EXAMPLE PARAGRAPH # 2

My Neighbor

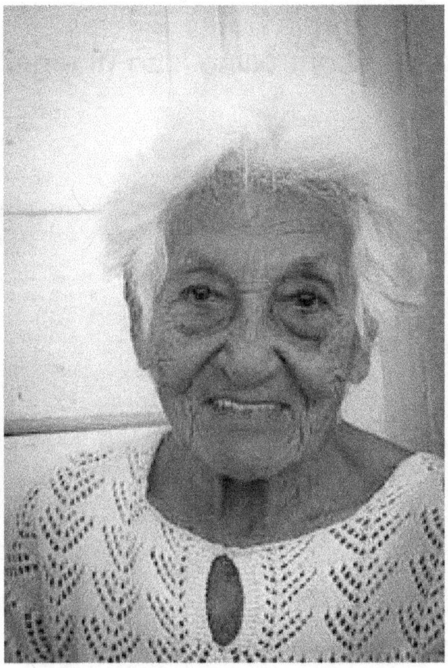

"Old Lady" by Theodor Hensolt is licensed under CC BY 2.0. To view a copy of this license, visit https://creativecommons.org/licenses/by/2.0/?ref=openverse.

My neighbor, Mrs. Morales, is 89-years-old, and she takes care of herself. She is very short and thin. She has a little dog. His name is Sam, and he barks a lot. She takes him on a walk 3 times a day. Mrs. Morales goes to the supermarket by herself and cooks all her food. She likes cooking and makes a very good tomato soup. Mrs. Morales even takes her heavy garbage out all by herself. When I am old, I hope I can do everything by myself like Mrs. Morales.

Activity 2

Underline the topic sentence.

1. What does Mrs. Morales do to take care of herself? ______________________

____

2. Underline the concluding sentence.
3. Do you like this paragraph? Why? Why not? ______________________

____

Important: In example paragraph # 1 and example paragraph # 2:

The paragraph has a title in the center of the page.
The beginning of the paragraph is indented.
The paragraph is double-spaced.

TOPIC SENTENCE

The topic sentence is the most important sentence in your paragraph. It has 2 parts:

1. Topic
2. Controlling idea (the general theme of the essay)

Example # 1:

"Central Park - Manhattan, New York" by Dougtone is licensed under CC BY-SA 2.0. https://creativecommons.org/licenses/by-sa/2.0/?ref=openverse.

Topic sentence: Central Park is a very fun place to visit.

1. Topic: "Central Park"

2. Controlling idea: "fun place to visit."

Example # 2

Topic sentence: My friend Jesse is beautiful and always happy.

1. Topic: "Jesse"

2. Controlling idea: "beautiful and happy."

"Close up portrait of happy and beautiful young woman relaxing enjoying the fresh beauty of gorgeous orange marigold flowers field in travel and holidays. Bali island." by Artem Beliaikin is marked with CC0 1.0. https://creativecommons.org/publicdomain/zero/1.0/?ref=openverse.

Activity 3

Write good topic sentences for these paragraphs.

My Brother

____

____

"Happy boy" by pedrosimoes7 is licensed under CC BY 2.0. https://creativecommons.org/licenses/by/2.0/?ref=openverse.

He is very tall and has short black hair and kind brown eyes. He always helps me. For example, he fixes my car when it does not work. He gives me good advice. He helped me decide to go to Kean University. He believes in me. He knows I am smart and I will be a good business woman. He is a loyal friend. If a friend tells him a secret, he will not share it with anyone. He is good to everyone. He often gives money to homeless people on the street. My brother is one of my best friends because he is kind and cares for me.

My Room

____

____

When I enter the door, I see a small window on the left. I can hear birds out the window in the spring and summer. Next to the window, there is a night table with a small lamp on it. The lamp gives a warm light to the room. On the other side of the bed there is another night table and lamp. Near the window is a shelf with a TV on top of it. The bed is big, and the blanket is blue and green. I love reading on my bed. On the ceiling of my room there is a fan with a light. It keeps my room cool in the summer. My room is my favorite place to relax in.

____

"Master Bedroom" by RyanGWU82 is licensed under CC BY 2.0.
https://creativecommons.org/licenses/by/2.0/?ref=openverse.

My Porch

____

____

There are two small tables and one chair in the center of my porch. I like to sit in the chair and read a book. I love plants, so there are flowers everywhere. Sometimes, I see rabbits and squirrels playing in my yard from my porch. There is a beautiful view of the sky. We often sit and eat dinner and watch the sun set. My porch is the most beautiful place in the world to me.

"Front Porch settin'" by rkramer62 is licensed under CC BY 2.0.
https://creativecommons.org/licenses/by/2.0/?ref=openverse.

SUPPORTING SENTENCES

Supporting sentences give details about the topic sentence. They explain why your topic sentence is true. These sentences are the biggest part of your paragraph.

Activity 4

1. Underline the supporting sentences in the 3 paragraphs in Activity 3 starting on page 7.

2. Write supporting sentences for these pictures from above:

Central Park is a very fun place to visit. ________________________________

"Central Park - Manhattan, New York" by Dougtone is licensed under CC BY-SA 2.0. https://creativecommons.org/licenses/by-sa/2.0/?ref=openverse.

____

____

____

____

____

____

____

____

I visit Central Park on the weekends with my family in good weather.

"Close up portrait of happy and beautiful young woman relaxing enjoying the fresh beauty of gorgeous orange marigold flowers field in travel and holidays. Bali island." by Artem Beliaikin is marked with CC0 1.0. https://creativecommons.org/publicdomain/zero/1.0/?ref=openverse.

My friend Jessie is beautiful and always happy.

I like spending time with my friend Jesse.

CONCLUDING SENTENCE

The concluding sentence is the last sentence in a paragraph. A concluding sentence repeats the main idea from the topic sentence in different words. It can also give your opinion of your subject.

Example # 1

Topic sentence: The café is beautiful and relaxing.

Concluding sentence: After a long day, drinking tea in the café takes away my stress.

"Coffee Shop" by TBoard is licensed under CC BY 2.0. https://creativecommons.org/licenses/by/2.0/?ref=openverse.

Example # 2

"Jason Straatmann Actor Model with Suit, Tie and Cufflinks" by satomodel is licensed under CC BY 2.0. https://creativecommons.org/licenses/by/2.0/?ref=openverse.

Topic sentence: My uncle George is selfish and mean.

Concluding sentence: Although my uncle George is not very nice, he likes to have fun.

WEAK PARAGRAPHS

Read the paragraphs below and decide what the problems are. Is it the topic sentence, the supporting sentences or the concluding sentence?

Paragraph # 1

My Office

"Disappointed Woman Working on Laptop" by userpilot1 is licensed under CC BY 2.0. https://creativecommons.org/licenses/by/2.0/?

My desk is in the middle of the room. My laptop is on my desk. I have a cup of coffee on my desk and my cell phone. My chair is behind my desk and it is very comfortable. Behind my chair is a wooden bookshelf. It has different objects in it. There is also a conference table for office meetings. My office has everything I need to be comfortable.

Paragraph # 2

My Best Friend

My best friend is very fun and nice. She has long, brown hair and dark brown eyes. She is from the Dominican Republic. I hope my best friend and I will always live in the same place because she is so kind.

"Young woman portrait" by sandro349 is marked with CC0 1.0. To view the terms, visit https://creativecommons.org/publicdomain/zero/1.0/?ref=openverse.

Paragraph # 3

Times Square is a busy and exciting place to visit. There are big, bright signs everywhere. It is never dark and you cannot see the stars at night. The sidewalks and roads are crowded. Taxis crowd the streets honking. Many tourists walk on the sidewalks. It is difficult to move quickly because of all the cars and people. Stores and restaurants are on every corner. The smell of good food is in the streets everywhere.

"TIME SQUARE" by airlines470 is licensed under CC BY-SA 2.0.
https://creativecommons.org/licenses/by-sa/2.0/?ref=openverse

Activity 5

1. What part(s) of paragraph # 1 is bad? (circle)
    a. Topic sentence
    b. Supporting sentences
    c. Concluding sentence

2. What part(s) of paragraph # 2 is bad? (circle)
    a. Topic sentence
    b. Supporting sentences
    c. Concluding sentence

3. What part(s) of paragraph # 3 is bad? (circle)
    a. Topic sentence
    b. Supporting sentences
    c. Concluding sentence

Choose one of these paragraphs and rewrite it in your notebook so it is stronger.

Activity 6

Describe your bedroom in your notebook. Use a topic sentence, supporting sentences and a concluding sentence.

Chapter 2: Descriptive Paragraph: People

EXAMPLE PARAGRAPH # 1

Erika Sanchez
ESL 0090-01
9/20/20___
3rd Draft: Descriptive Paragraph: Person

My Classmate

My new classmate, Juan, is a friendly, cheerful and likeable person. He is from the Dominican Republic. He has lived in New Jersey for three years. He is tall and slim. He has short, dark and curly hair. He wears casual, comfortable clothes to class. He studies English for one hour every day. His major is Computer Science. Now, he works in a supermarket. He is a cashier. His favorite hobby is baseball. He likes watching it and playing it. He is fit because he plays baseball. His favorite food is rice, beans and chicken. In English class, Juan always tells jokes. He is also a good student and helps other students. Our class is more interesting because of him, and I am glad he is here.

"Maël (suite...)" by Grégoire Lannoy is licensed under CC BY 2.0. https://creativecommons.org/licenses/by/2.0/?ref=openverse.

<u>**Activity 1**</u>

Answer these questions about the paragraph above:

1. Who is the author describing? ____

____

2. What does the author's classmate look like? ______________________________

____

3. What are some personality traits of the author's classmate? ____________________

____

4. How does the author feel about her classmate? ____________________________

____

DESCRIBING PEOPLE: ADJECTIVES

When you describe people, you can describe what they look like on the **outside** (their appearance), and what they are like on the **inside** (their personality).

Outside

Here are some useful words to describe a person's outward appearance:

General	Beautiful, average, ugly
Body	Fat, large, skinny, fit, short, medium-height, tall
Skin	Fair, black, brown
Eyes	Brown, black, blue, green hazel, small, big
Age	Young, middle-aged, old
Hair	Blonde, brunette, red, black, bald, short, long, curly, straight
Clothing	Casual, formal, elegant, comfortable

When we describe someone's outward appearance, we often use the verbs: "to be" and "to have."

For example:

1. My daughter Olivia is young and happy.
2. She is very beautiful.
3. Olivia is three years old.
4. She has long, brown hair, and she has big, brown eyes.
5. She is short and her skin is light brown.
6. She likes stuffed animals.
7. She has a lot of jewelry and wears it every day.
8. She will be a beautiful, strong woman when she grows up.

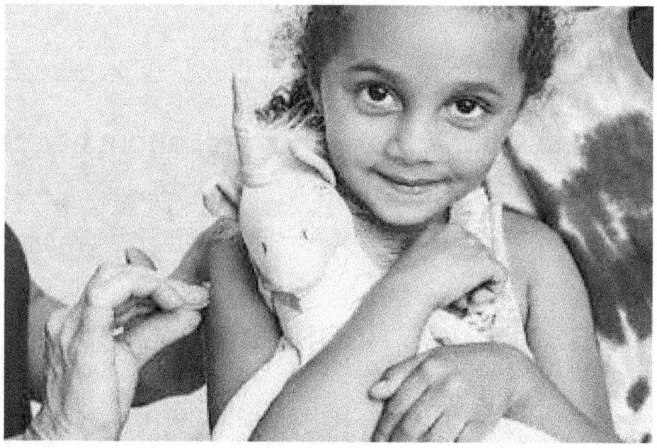

Activity 2

Circle the "to be" verbs and underline the "to have" verbs in the sentences above.

Activity 3

Write 5 sentences about this person's outward appearance in your notebook using the verbs "to be" and "to have".

Inside

In the descriptive paragraph, you also need to describe what the person is like on the inside. Here is a useful list of words to describe people's personalities:

Angry	Brave	Calm	Caring
Cheerful	Dependable	Easy-going	Energetic
Friendly	Funny	Generous	Hard-working
Helpful	Impatient	Intelligent	Interesting
Kind	Lazy	Mature	Nervous
Patient	Proud	Quiet	Sad
Serious	Shy	Thoughtful	Thoughtless
Unhappy			

Activity 4

Complete the following activities:

1. Circle the words in the box that are negative.
2. Underline the words in the box that are positive.
3. Write down 3 positive words that describe you.
4. Write down 3 negative words that describe you.

Activity 5

Write a small paragraph describing yourself--both outside and inside.

PREWRITNG

"Pre" = before.

Prewriting is writing ideas before you write your paragraph. Prewriting helps you think of all the details about your subject. For the descriptive paragraph about a person, we use mind mapping.

For example:

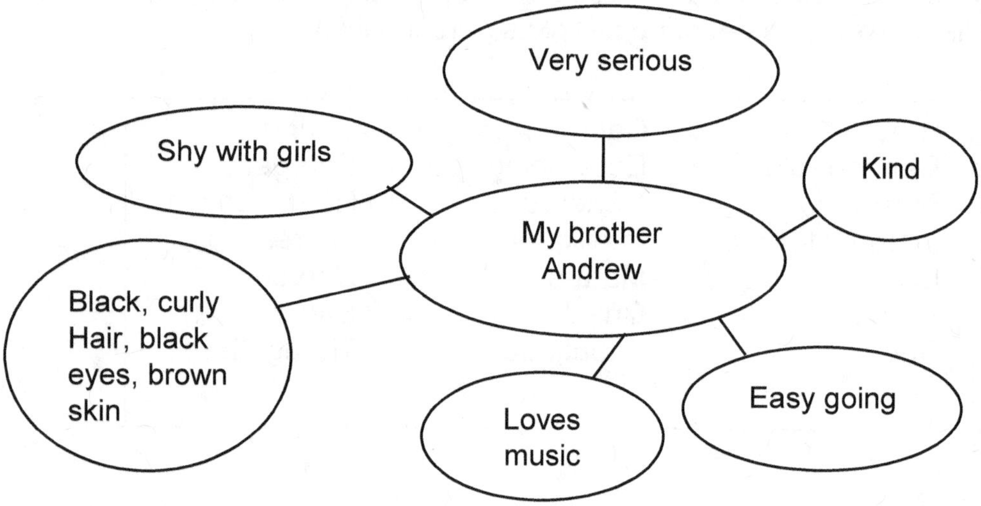

After you spend time writing all the ideas you can think of about your subject, you want to decide what are the best ideas. Now, you cross off the ideas that are not strong, and add more details to the best ideas.

For example:

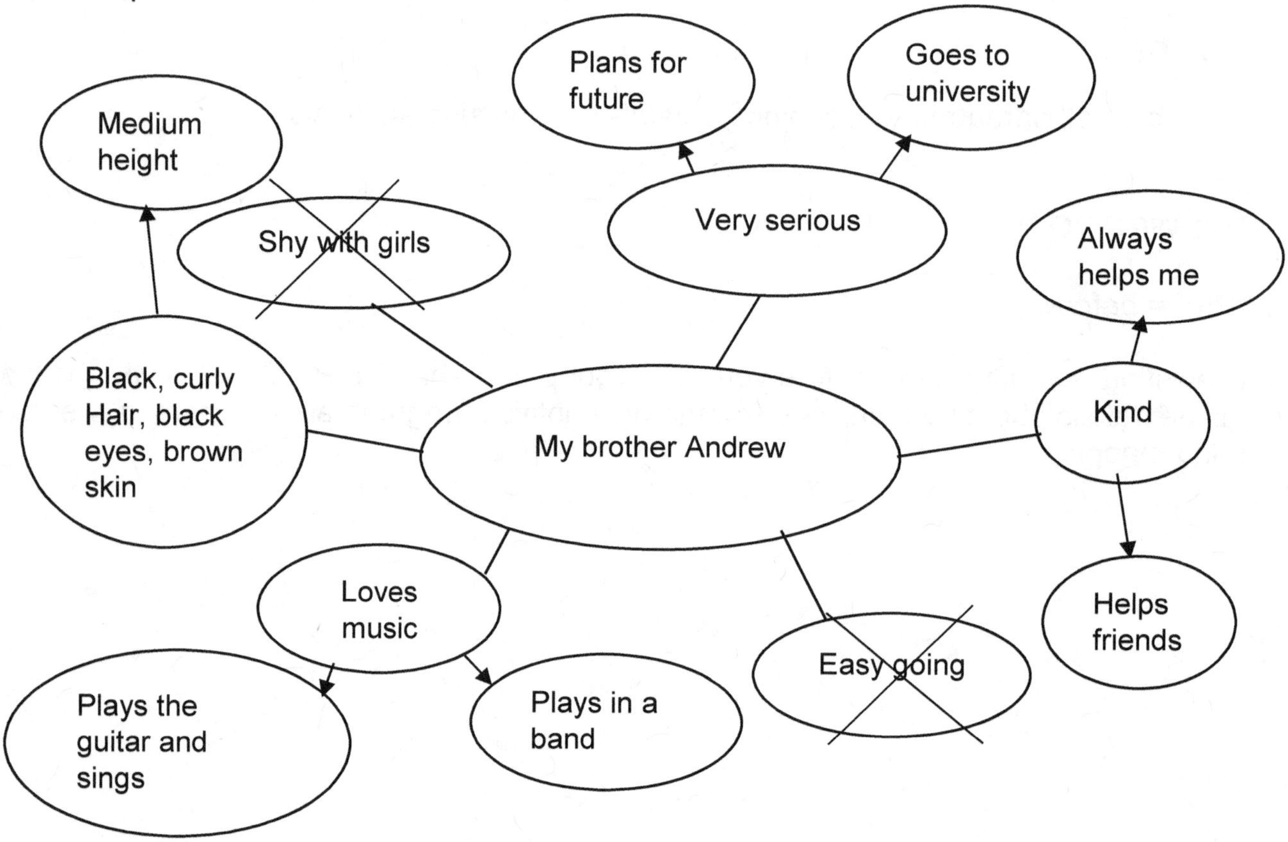

Activity 6

Choose a family member. In your notebook, create a mind map like the above examples.

TOPIC SENTENCE

The topic sentence is the most important sentence in a paragraph. This sentence gives the main idea of the paragraph. A topic sentence has 2 parts:

1. The topic: Who the paragraph is about
2. The controlling idea: The general characteristics of the person

For example: (the topic is in bold, and the controlling idea is underlined)

My mother <u>is the wisest person I know</u>.

My mother <u>is a beautiful person both outside and inside</u>.

<u>Strict, but fun are the main character traits that describe</u> **my mother.**

In the sentences above, the topic is the same. The controlling idea changes. The topic can come before or after the controlling idea.

Activity 7

Read the following topic sentences. Circle the topic and underline the controlling idea:

1. My classmate George is an interesting person.
2. Challenging and nice are the perfect words to describe my English Teacher.
3. My brother Kas is small, but full of energy.
4. My mother is the best mom in the world.
5. My son is a cute and happy person.

Activity 8

Finish these topic sentences about people you know. What are the most important characteristics of the following people?

1. My grandmother ______________________________

____

2. My cousin ______________________________

____

3. My math teacher ______________________________

____

CONCLUDING SENTENCE

The concluding sentence is the last sentence in a paragraph. A concluding sentence says the main idea again in different words. It can give your final thoughts of your subject too.

Compare the following topic and concluding sentences in the chart below.

Topic sentence	Concluding Sentence(s)
My mother is the wisest person I know.	My mother is very wise, and I cannot imagine my life without her.
My mother is a beautiful person both inside and out.	My mother is beautiful and she has a great personality. I am happy to be her daughter.
Strict, but compassionate are the main character traits that describe my mother	My mother loves to laugh, but she is a good discipliner too. I think this is the best combination for the perfect mother.

Activity 9

Practice writing concluding sentences for these topic sentences.

Topic Sentence	Concluding Sentence
My classmate George is an interesting person.	
Challenging and nice are the perfect adjectives to describe my English teacher.	
My brother Kas is small, but full of energy.	
My mother is the best mom in the world.	
My son is a cute and happy person.	

Activity 10

Reread Example Paragraph # 1 on page 14. Answer the questions:

1. Identify the topic sentence and the concluding sentence.
2. What are some details that the author uses to describe her classmate?

EXAMPLE PARAGRAPH # 2

(From the prewriting on page 18)

Juana Castillo
ESL 0090-01
9/20/20____
3rd Draft: Descriptive Paragraph: Person

My Brother

My older brother, Andrew, has a very kind but serious personality. He is medium height and has short, black, curly hair and black eyes. His skin is brown. Andrew really loves music. He started playing the guitar when he was 7-years-old. Now, he plays in a band with his best friend. He is very serious about his future. He does not go to parties. He goes to Kean University and studies music. He has many plans for when he graduates. He wants to teach music. My brother is also very kind. When I need help with my homework, he helps me. He also tries to protect me from boys that like me. I do not like this, but I appreciate his heart. He helps his friends too. My brother is a wonderful person.

Activity 11

1. Write the topic sentence in the above paragraph: ______________________

____

2. What is the main idea of the paragraph:

   a. My brother likes music.

   b. My brother is an interesting person.

   c. My brother has black hair.

3. What are 3 details that the author uses to support her main idea?

a. ____

____

b. ____

____

c. ____

____

4. Write the concluding sentence: ____________________

____

Activity 12

Review the prewriting mind map about a family member you completed in Activity 6. Write a paragraph about this family member. Use a topic sentence and a concluding sentence.

WRITING ASSIGNMENT

Write a paragraph about a person you know (minimum 125 words)

Step 1: Topic

Below is a list of topic ideas. You may use one of these, or ask your instructor about a different idea:

Your best friend
A person you admire
Someone you miss
A classmate

Step 2: Prewrite

Use the prewriting steps on page 17 to get ideas about your topic.

Step 3: First Draft

Use your prewriting to help write the first draft of your descriptive paragraph. When you are finished, ask a classmate to read your paragraph and give you advice. Include topic and concluding sentences.

Chapter 3: Descriptive Paragraph: Places

EXAMPLE PARAGRAPH # 1

Nicole Hernandez
0090-01
10/03/20___
3rd Draft Descriptive Paragraph: Place

My Bedroom

My bedroom is the most private space I have, and it is relaxing and comfortable. It is the place where I can rest and sleep peacefully. My room is painted light gray and pink. It has a very rich smell because I have a pineapple air freshener. There are two big windows in my room. I can hear cars driving by from my window. In the front of my room, I have a large, white mirror. Next to the mirror, I have a small fan. I have a black floor lamp on the other side of the mirror. In the middle of my room, I have my bed. It is a queen size, and it is mahogany. My bed is very comfortable, and on top of my bed, I have two pillows that are soft and fluffy. There is a closet, where I have all my clothes, and my shoes are in front of my bed. In the back of my room, I have a mahogany dresser, where I keep my intimate clothes and my accessories. On top of my dresser, I have perfume and many different creams; each one has a rich fragrance. My room is beautiful and comfortable.

Activity 1

Answer the questions.

1. Where is the topic sentence? Underline the topic sentence.
2. Where is the concluding sentence? Underline the concluding sentence.
3. How does the writer feel about her room?

THE FIVE SENSES
In descriptive writing, it is very important to use the five senses.
What are the five senses?

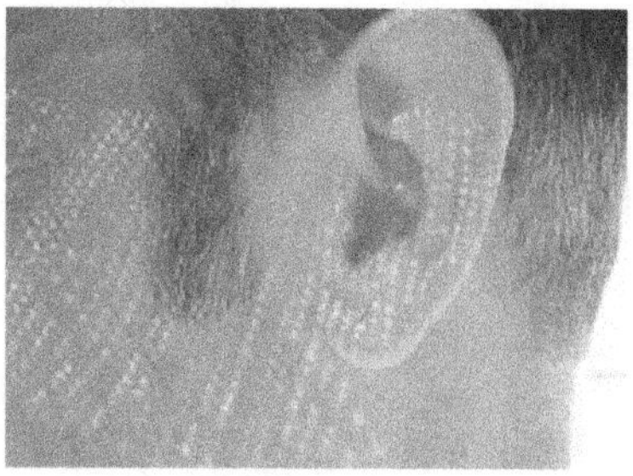

"Ear" by Menage a Moi is licensed under CC BY-SA 2.0. https://creativecommons.org/licenses/by-sa/2.0/?ref=openverse.

"Eye Retouch" by Agnes_F is licensed under CC BY-ND 2.0. https://creativecommons.org/licenses/by-nd/2.0/?ref=openverse.

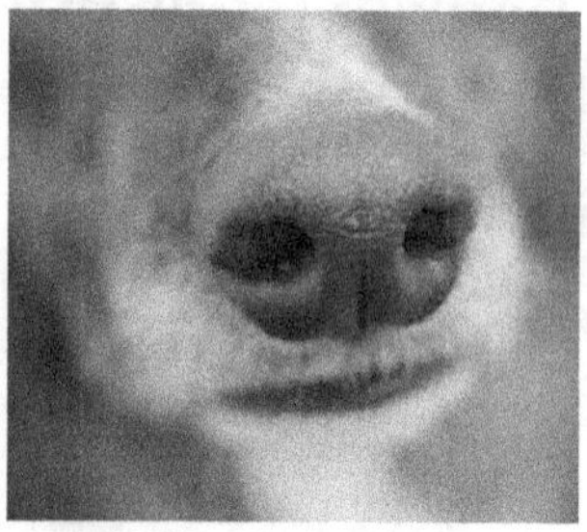

"N is for Nose - E X P L O R E D" by Clint__Budd is licensed under CC BY 2.0. https://creativecommons.org/licenses/by/2.0/?ref=openverse.

"Eating ice cream" by nvainio is licensed under CC BY 2.0. https://creativecommons.org/licenses/by/2.0/?ref=openverse.

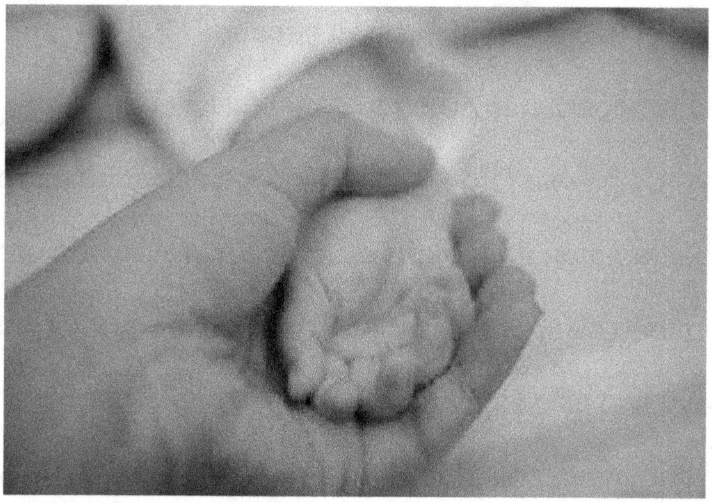

"Little hand" by ePi.Longo is licensed under CC BY-SA 2.0. To view a copy of this license, visit https://creativecommons.org/licenses/by-sa/2.0/?ref=openverse.

Activity 2

1. Look at the pictures above and write the 5 senses:

   1. ____________________
   2. ____________________
   3. ____________________
   4. ____________________
   5. ____________________

2. What senses does the author use in Example Paragraph # 1? ____________________

____

DESCRIPTIVE ADJECTIVES

Taste	Touch	Sight	Sound	Smell
delicious	smooth	beautiful	loud	delicious
sweet	soft	ugly	noisy	fresh
salty	rough	dark	silent	stinky
juicy	hard	bright	quiet	smelly
hot	heavy	colorful	laughing	sweet
cold	light	clean	screaming	dirty
spicy	cold	messy		fragrant
horrible	hot	small		strong
	sticky	big		
	warm	busy		
		old		
		shiny		
		tall		
		elegant		

Activity 3

What senses would you use to describe the below objects/people? What adjectives would you use?

a. *Ex: Sunset on a beach:* *Sight: Beautiful, colorful (orange, pink, red, yellow).*

Touch: Warm soft sand, the breeze. Smell: Salty water.

b. Dog: ____

____

c. Pizza: ____

____

d. Bed: ____

____

e. Baby: ____

____

f. Park: ____

Activity 4

1. Think of a room in your house. What adjectives would you use to describe this room?

____

____

2. Think of a favorite place outside. What adjectives would you use to describe this place?

____

____

PREPOSITIONS

in front of	next to	on the left/right of
under	behind	above
below	between	inside
near	on	in back of
in the middle of		

Activity 5

Complete the sentences with prepositions from the box above (more than one preposition is possible).

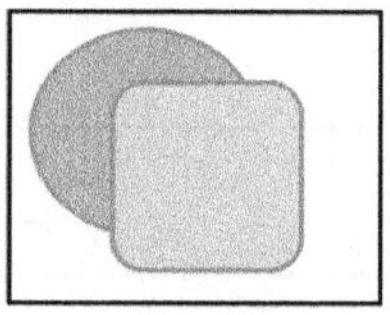

1. The square is ________________ the circle.
2. The circle is __________________ the square.

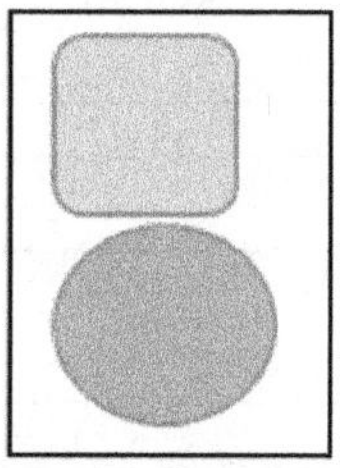

3. The circle is _________________ the square.
4. The square is _________________ the circle.

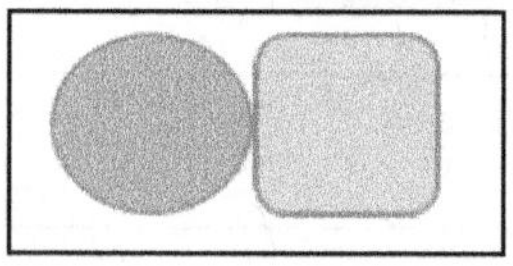

5. The circle is ________________ the square.
6. The square is _______________ the circle.

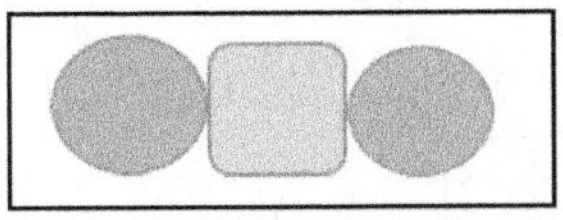

7. The square is ________________ the circles.

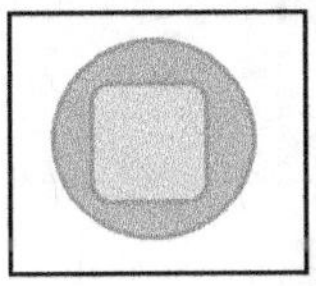

8. The square is ____________ the circle.

Activity 6

Write 5 descriptive sentences about the following pictures using prepositions.

"Peggy's Zen living room makeover, white sofa, pink tulips, bright pillows, maroon throw, natural woven drum shaped tables, jute rug, refinished floor, old brass floor lamp, Seattle, Washington, USA" To view a copy of this license, visit https://creativecommons.org/licenses/by/2.0/?ref=openverse.

EX: *The sofa in front of the lamp.*

1. ______________________________

2. ______________________________

3. ______________________________

4. ______________________________

5. ______________________________

"Central Park" by ZeroOne is licensed under CC BY-SA 2.0. https://creativecommons.org/licenses/by-sa/2.0/?ref=openverse.

EX: There are tall buildings behind the park.

1. ______________________________

2. ______________________________

3. ______________________________

4. ______________________________

5. ______________________________

TOPIC SENTENCE

When you write a descriptive paragraph about a place, it is important to include a topic sentence.

There are 2 parts of the topic sentence:

1. The topic: The place you are describing
2. The controlling idea: A general description of the place (i.e.: Beautiful, fun, exciting, messy etc...)

For example:

Sunset beach is an attractive, lively beach in southern New Jersey.

My room is a quiet, yet messy place.

The classroom is a comfortable place to learn.

Activity 7

Circle the topic and underline the controlling idea in the topic sentences above.

CONCLUDING SENTENCE

The concluding sentence can repeat the ideas from the topic sentence in different words and/or give the writer's opinion or feeling about the topic.

For example:

Sunset beach is a great place to go for the day with your family.

Although it is small and messy, my room is a great place to relax and study.

Our classroom is a peaceful and cheerful place to learn.

Activity 8

Circle the topic and underline the controlling idea in the concluding sentences above.

EXAMPLE PARAGRAPH # 2

Jorge Morales
10/03/20_____
3rd Draft: Descriptive Paragraph: Place

My Dream House

My dream house in Miami, Florida is big and beautiful. It is perfect for any activity. I can go for a walk, or swim whenever I want to at my dream house. Outside the house, there is a beautiful yard and six garages for all of my cars and for my friends to come visit. In the back, there is a gorgeous pool, and you can see a beautiful view of the beach from the pool patio. In the morning, you can see the sunrise on the water and hear birds singing in the palm trees. I have a modern grill next to the pool where I make barbecue for my family and friends every weekend. My barbecue is delicious and spicy.

Inside the house on the first floor, there is a big living room, which is relaxing and always neat. There is a big, comfortable sofa in the middle, and a TV on the wall. I have my PS4 near the TV too. The living room smells clean and fresh. Next to the living room, there is a dining room, and in front of the dining room is a large kitchen, because my mom visits a lot and likes to cook. It always smells like Cuban food in there. On the second floor of my dream house, there are three bedrooms. The master bedroom has a walk-in closet, and I have a beautiful king-size bed that is very soft. Next to the bed, there is a white nightstand with a modern-looking lamp. The other two bedrooms are for guests. Each bedroom has its own bathroom, and the color is white. The second floor is bright and cheerful. I love my dream house, and I am going to work hard for this. If you can dream it, you can have it.

Activity 9

Complete the following activities:

1. Underline the topic and concluding sentences.
2. Circle the prepositions.
3. Circle the descriptive adjectives.
4. Write some examples of sensory details the author writes about:

   Sight: ____

   Sound: ____

   Smell: ____

   Taste: ____

   Touch: ____

5. How does the author feel about his dream house? ____________________

____

PREWRITING

Prewriting is writing down all the ideas you can think of about your subject before you write a paragraph.

To describe a place, listing is a good technique.

For example:

Paragraph Title: My Living Room

Front of the Room

(What do I see, hear, taste, smell, touch? What adjectives can I use to describe it?)

- Carpet (white, thick)
- Desk (old, gold, wooden)

Middle of the Room

(What do I see, hear, taste, smell, touch? What adjectives can I use to describe it?)

- Fragrant flowers on the table
- Sofas, chairs and pillows (soft)
- Glass table (shiny)
- Ceiling light (big, elegant)

Back of the Room

- Fireplace (hot)
- Windows (bright, tall)
- Piano (music)
- Curtains (long, gray)
- Mirror (large, gold)

"Villa Sienna living room" by Gatsby's List is licensed under CC BY-ND 2.0. https://creativecommons.org/licenses/by-nd/2.0/?ref=openverse.

When you finish your prewriting, you can write your paragraph:

EXAMPLE PARAGRAPH # 3

David Mendez
10/10/20____
3rd Draft: Descriptive Paragraph: Place

My Living Room

My living room is a bright and comfortable space. There is a white carpet that covers most of the floor. It is thick, and it makes the space feel cozy. In the front, there is a wooden desk with gold accents. The desk is very old and I write letters there. In the middle of the room, there are soft, comfortable white sofas and chairs. I like to take a nap on the sofa on the weekends. A bright elegant light is above the sofa and chairs. In the center of the room, near the sofa there is a shiny glass table. I always put flowers on the table, so that the room smells fragrant. In the back of the room, there is a fireplace. In the winter, I like to have hot fires that make the living room warm and welcoming. Above the fireplace is a large gold mirror. On the right side of the fireplace, there are two tall bright windows. The windows have long gray curtains on them. Between the windows is a black piano. I like to play loud music and the piano sounds beautiful. My living room is a great space to relax and feel at home.

Activity 10

Complete the following activities:

1. Underline the topic and concluding sentences.

2. Write some examples of sensory details the author writes about:

   Sight: ____

   Sound: ____

Smell: ____

Taste: ____

Touch: ____

3. How does the author feel about his living room? ____________________

____

4. What is your favorite part of this paragraph? ______________________

____

WRITING ASSIGNMENT

Write a descriptive paragraph about a place that is special to you (Minimum 200 words)

Step 1: Topic

Below is a list of topic ideas. You may use one of these, or ask your instructor about a different idea:

A room in your house (not your bedroom)
A favorite park
A favorite place to hang out with friends
A place on campus that you like

Step 2: Prewrite

Create a list like the one on page 33 to get ideas about your topic.

Step 3: First Draft

Use your prewriting to help write the first draft of your descriptive paragraph. You should follow your ideas from your prewrite as you work on your first draft.

When you are finished with your first draft, go through the following checklist:

1. Does my topic sentence clearly state what I will describe? Do I have a concluding sentence?
2. Do my supporting sentences have enough details?
3. Did I use sensory details other than "sight?"
4. Did I write at least 150 words?

*It is a good idea to have a classmate read your paragraph and give you advice.

Chapter 4: Narrative Paragraph

"Narrative" means "story." A narrative paragraph tells the story of an event.

We hear narratives everyday:

- Movies
- Netflix series
- Novels (books)
- History
- Family stories
- Stories from your life you tell friends

Activity 1

Ask and answer these questions with a classmate:

1. What was the name of a recent movie you saw? What was it about?
2. What was your graduation day like? What happened?

What is a Narrative Paragraph?

- It tells a story from your life or from the life of someone else.
- It has a topic and concluding sentence.
- It often shares the person's feelings about the event.
- It mostly uses the past simple verb tense.

EXAMPLE PARAGRAPH # 1

Juliana Padilla
ESL 0090-01
9/30/______
3rd Draft Narrative Paragraph

Pool Rescue

It is a great experience rescuing someone from harm. Last summer, my family went to a park to have a nice time together. It was a very hot day. After we ate lunch, my cousin Maria and I decided to go to the pool and swim. We had a lot of fun in the water, but something strange on the other side of the pool caught our attention. We saw a boy in the pool, and it was too deep for him. He was alone and he began to sink. His arms were moving frantically above his head. My cousin and I were the closest to him, and we swam to him quickly. Then, we grabbed his arms and pulled him out of the water. Instantly, the lifeguards came to give him first aid. The lifeguards tried helping him with CPR, but the boy did not react. All the people at the pool were very scared. The boy's mother did not stop crying and praying to God. After a minute, the boy opened his eyes, and an ambulance immediately took him to the hospital. I did not find out anything more about that child, but I can say that it has marked my life. I have an 8-year-old brother and he is not a good swimmer. When we go to the pool or the beach, I watch him carefully when he swims. I do not want to repeat that moment. I will never forget the day I helped this boy from drowning.

"public swimming pool @ annecy France - WP_20150806_17_45_46_Pro" by Nicola since 1972 is licensed under CC BY 2.0. visit https://creativecommons.org/licenses/by/2.0/?ref=openverse.

Activity 2

1. Underline the topic and concluding sentence.
2. When did this story take place? ______________________________

____

3. Where did the story take place? ______________________________

____

4. Underline all the past simple verbs you see in this paragraph.
5. How does the author feel about this event? ______________________

____

PREWRITING

Before you write a narrative paragraph, it is important to organize the events in the story. What happens first? What happens after that? Writing a list with the order of events can be helpful.

For example, below is a list of notes from example paragraph # 1:

Got up
Packed lunches
Went to the park with family—my mother, father, brother, sister, my cousin, aunt, uncle.
Cousin and I decided to swim
We had fun, but then saw something bad.
Little boy--drowning
We pulled him out of the water
Life guards—CPR
Hospital
Went back to my family
Watch my brother swimming

Activity 3

Answer the questions about the prewriting:

1. Circle the details from the prewriting that the author used in the example paragraph.
2. Cross out the details from the prewriting that the author did not use in the example paragraph.

When you list for a narrative, you write down all of your ideas in time order. Then you decide what details to use for your paragraph.

EXAMPLE PARAGRAPH # 2

Listing Prewriting:

Got up
Nervous
Airport
Plane ride—bumpy
Landed in Newark
Saw my family—nieces for the 1st time
Got in the car—outside looked so different
American restaurant—colors blue and white
Delicious food, great service
Went to bed, and slept late
Went to an amusement park with family
Waterpark
Ate lunch—hotdogs—they didn't taste good
Rode some other rides
Big roller coaster—I was nervous, but it was my favorite.
I ate ice cream
We went home, my nieces slept in the car

Felix Rodriguez
ESL 0090-01
11/20/_____
3rd Draft Narrative Paragraph

My First Day in the United States

Living the American dream was something I always thought about in my country. Then, a few years ago, I got the chance to come to the United States. After a long preparation process, we finally landed in Newark Airport. I met my family, my sister, her husband, and my two beautiful nieces, Juliana and Michelle, 2 and 4 years old. This was my first time meeting my nieces. It was very emotional to see them and to hug them. Next, we went to a restaurant. There we ate traditional American food. The moment I tried that food, it became my favorite. It tasted delicious. It was a super nice restaurant. It was very private since it had about 10 small tables. The service was perfect, and the music playing was fabulous. The next day we went to a large amusement park. There I had fun with my little nieces. There were different types of activities in the park. I remember there was a very big water park. I slid quickly down slides with my nieces. Then we went to look at the rides. I saw a very tall roller coaster. I was very scared to ride it, but my parents promised that if I ride, they would buy me a delicious sweet. I finally decided to ride that roller coaster. I liked it so much; I rode it three times in a row. Without a doubt, the first 24 hours of my stay in the United States was excellent.

"Ingoldmells roller-coaster" by ☺ Lee J Haywood is licensed under CC BY-SA 2.0. visit https://creativecommons.org/licenses/by-sa/2.0/?ref=openverse.

Activity 4

When you are finished reading example paragraph # 2, answer the following questions:

1. Look at the prewriting list. Circle the details the author chose to use in his paragraph.
2. Look at the prewriting list. Cross out the details the author did NOT use in his paragraph. Why do you think he did not use these ideas?
3. Underline the topic and concluding sentences in the paragraph.
4. Underline the simple past verb forms in the paragraph.
5. How does the author feel about this event?

Activity 5

1. Look at the pictures on the next page about graduation day—they are in chronological order.

2. Take turns with your partner describing the pictures.

3. How is this graduation day story the same as the day you graduated from high school?

4. How is this graduation day story different from the day you graduated?

"Yuno's alarm clock ? No, it's mine." by matsuyuki is licensed under CC BY-SA 2.0. https://creativecommons.org/licenses/by-sa/2.0/?ref=openverse.

"Breakfast" by Charles Haynes is licensed under CC BY-SA 2.0. https://creativecommons.org/licenses/by-sa/2.0/?ref=openverse.

"2012 Hyundai i30 - First Drive - NRMA New Cars" by The National Roads and Motorists' Association is licensed under CC BY 2.0. https://creativecommons.org/licenses/by/2.0/?ref=openverse.

"New York City, Manhattan, Little Italy : ' Hair Salon '" by (vincent desjardins) is licensed under CC BY 2.0. https://creativecommons.org/licenses/by/2.0/?ref=openverse.

"Graduation" by schwglr is licensed under CC BY-SA 2.0. https://creativecommons.org/licenses/by-sa/2.0/?ref=openverse.

"Graduation" by robb3d is licensed under CC BY 2.0. https://creativecommons.org/licenses/by/2.0/?ref=openverse.

"Graduation party decor" by eliud51 is licensed under CC BY-ND 2.0. https://creativecommons.org/licenses/by-nd/2.0/?ref=openverse.

Activity 6

Look at the pictures again.

1. Prewrite a list of the order of events in this story.
2. Write a paragraph about this story.

TRANSITIONS

In a narrative paragraph, it is important to use words that move the story along so that your reader knows the story is changing. Here are some transition signals useful for narrative writing:

First, one day

Second, third

Then, after that, after a while, next

Now, at this time, during

Immediately, soon

In the morning (afternoon, evening, summer, etc...)

At 12:00

The next day (week, month, year)

Finally, at last

Activity 7

Circle the transition words in example essay # 1 and example essay # 2.

Activity 8

Fill in the blank with transition words in the paragraph below.

One day	Then	When
After a while	25 minutes later	Finally

My First Lie

The first time I remember lying to my parents, I was 8 years old. When I was a little boy, I was very curious and mischievous. I always wanted to play with my friends. ___________, I wanted to go outside and play, but that morning, the news spoke of a big storm in the afternoon. Because I was very naughty, I did not listen to the news. That afternoon, I told my mom that I would go to sleep in my room. ___________ when she was not looking, I escaped through the window, and I looked for my friends. ___________ I found them, we started to play and have fun. We did not think about the serious problem of the storm coming. As we started playing, raindrops began falling on us. We did not stop playing. ___________, hail started falling. It hurt when it fell on our heads and we got scared. My friends and I started to run when the lightning came. Bright light flashed across the dark gray sky, which made us even more afraid. We were alone, soaking wet and cold. We could not go home because our parents would get mad at us, so we hid under a bridge in the road. ___________we heard a van coming down the road and stopping. My friend Jose looked to see who it was, and thankfully it was our parents. They were very upset at us because we could have been badly injured by the storm. ___________ we got home, my mother punished me for one week; I could not see my friends. This experience taught me a great lesson. Lies are very harmful, especially lying to my parents.

TOPIC SENTENCE

A narrative paragraph needs a topic sentence. There are 2 parts of a topic sentence:

1. Topic
2. Controlling idea

In narrative writing, the **topic** is the event, or the name of the experience.

For example:

A skydiving lesson
My 10th birthday party
My vacation to Paris
The first day of university
Last Christmas

The **controlling idea** is a general description of the event.

For example:

A skydiving lesson was the best birthday gift my girlfriend could give me.

I had so much fun at my 10th birthday.

My vacation to Paris was hot and uncomfortable, but also amazing.

I got completely lost on the first day of university.

I will always remember Christmas last year as the last time I saw my grandmother.

Activity 9

Circle the topic and underline the controlling idea in the above topic sentences.

Activity 10

More practice: Circle the topic and underline the controlling idea in the below sentences.

1. My 15th birthday party was the best day of my life.

2. Our high school prom was a very special event.

3. The day my nephew was born was unforgettable.

4. I felt so accomplished when I graduated from high school.

5. The first concert I went to was thrilling.

CONCLUDING SENTENCE

The concluding sentence also has a topic and a controlling idea. The concluding sentence in a narrative can:

1. Restate the topic sentence
2. Give the author's feelings about the event
   And/or
3. Tell what is happening now because of an event

For example:

Topic Sentence	Concluding Sentence
1. I had so much fun at my 10th birthday party.	*My 10th birthday party was full of fun and surprises. (restate the topic)*
2. My vacation to Paris was hot and uncomfortable, but also amazing.	*Paris was wonderful and I want to visit again soon. (author's feelings)*
3. I felt so accomplished when I graduated from high school.	*Now, I am attending Kean University and majoring in Business. I will always be grateful for my high school experience. (what is happening now, author's feelings)*
4. I got completely lost on the first day of university.	
5. The day my nephew was born was unforgettable.	
6. A skydiving lesson was the best birthday gift my girlfriend could give me.	
7. Our high school prom was a very special event.	

Activity 11

Practice writing concluding sentences for numbers 4-7 above.

NARRATIVE PARAGRAPH WRITING ASSIGNMENT

Write a narrative paragraph about an important day in your life (Minimum 250 words)

Step 1: Topic - Choose an important day in your life. Here are some ideas:

• The day you graduated from high school • Your first day in the United States • The day you won an award	• A big game you played in • A wedding day • The birth of a baby in your family

If there is time in class, describe the important event you chose to a partner.

Step 2: Prewrite

Once you choose a topic, prewrite ideas using the listing method on page 39. Try to list everything that happened on that day.

When you are done with your list, decide what information is most important for the topic. Cross out any information that is not important.

Step 3: First Draft

Write your first draft. Make sure your first draft includes:

- Title
- Topic sentence
- Enough details for your reader to understand what happened
- Your feelings on this day
- Concluding sentence to end your paragraph

*It is a good idea to ask someone to read your paragraph (a classmate is best) to make sure your story is clear.

Checklist for a narrative:

1. Does my topic sentence clearly state what my story is about? Do I have a concluding sentence?
2. Does my story have enough details in it for the reader to understand?
3. Did I use sensory details?
4. Did I use enough descriptive words?
5. Did I use transition signals?
6. Did I write at least 250 words?

Chapter 5: Sentence Structure

What is a sentence?

1. A group of words that expresses a complete idea.
2. Begins with a capital letter and ends in a period, exclamation point or a question mark.
3. Has a **subject** and a **verb**.

SUBJECT

The **subject** can be a noun (i.e. *Sandy, students, dog, New York City,* etc....) or a subject pronoun (i.e. *he, she, it* or *they*)

For example:

S
Sandy eats cake. or S
She eats cake.

Activity 1

Underline and label the subject in each sentence.

S
Ex: Mark goes to school every day.

1. My sisters are my best friends.
2. The apple was delicious.
3. It is going to rain all day.
4. They are coming for dinner tomorrow.
5. The class did not understand the teacher.
6. I love my dog.
7. The cat caught a mouse.
8. You are invited to my party.
9. She feels cold in the winter.

VERB

The **verb** comes after the subject in the sentence. It describes the action (i.e. *eat, play, read, have/has* etc…)

For example:

S V
Sandy eats cake.

S V
John has a cat.

S V
It is hot outside today.

Activity 2

Underline and label the subject and double underline and label the verb in each sentence:

1. He speaks Spanish well.
2. The students are beginners in this class.
3. Daniel runs to his class every day.
4. Our family has a big dog.
5. I am from Cuba.
6. Our class starts at 10:00 am on Mondays, Wednesdays and Fridays.
7. My mother likes chocolate.
8. The students study together on Tuesdays.
9. The Dominican Republic has many beautiful beaches.
10. The chair is next to the table.

STATEMENTS AND QUESTIONS

Some English sentences are **statements,** and some are **questions.**

Questions	**Statements**
How old are you?	I am 19 years old.
Where do you live?	I live in Newark.
Do you speak Spanish?	I speak Spanish.
Is he your best friend?	Yes, he is my best friend.
Do you like my car?	Yes, I like your car!

Statement:

- Starts with a capital letter, ends in a period or exclamation point (. or !)
- The subject comes first before the verb.

Question:

- Starts with a capital letter and ends in a question mark (?).
- The verb comes before the subject, or the subject is between the verbs.

Activity 3

Underline and label the subjects, double underline and label the verbs.

V S
Ex: How old are you?

S V
Ex: I am 19 years old.

V S V
Ex: Where do you live?

S V
Ex: I live in Newark.

1. Do you speak Spanish?
2. I speak Spanish.
3. Is he your best friend?
4. Yes, he is my best friend.
5. Do you like my car?
6. Yes, I like your car!

Activity 4

Statements: Put the words in order. Make sure you capitalize the first word and put a period at the end of each sentence.

1. live / we / on campus ______________________________
2. I / the piano / play ______________________________
3. hard / work / my classmates / on the homework ______________________________
4. eats / treats / my dog / after his walk ______________________________
5. from / he / Ecuador / is ______________________________
6. plays / Felix / soccer / every weekend ______________________________
7. on their lesson plans / the teachers / hard / work ______________________________
8. 2 brothers / Dorota / and / 1 sister / has ______________________________
9. to go / dancing / like / we ______________________________
10. is / the cake / very good ______________________________

Activity 5

Questions: Put the words in order. Make sure you capitalize the first word and put a question mark at the end of each sentence.

1. are / from / where / you ______________________________

____

2. English / you / speak / do ______________________________

____

3. how many / sisters / do / brothers / and / have / you ______________________________

____

4. drink / tea / you / do ______________________________

____

5. every day / do / watch / Netflix / you ______________________________

____

6. our class / does / when / meet ______________________________

____

7. Jose / Bachata / does / like ______________________________

____

8. at the door / is / who ______________________________

____

9. have / your roommate / a lot of books / does ______________________________

____

10. your name / is / what ______________________________

____

CAPITALIZATION RULES

Here are some capitalization rules in English:

Capitalize…	**Examples**
the first word of every sentence and the pronoun "I"	My friend and I watch a movie every Friday night. Do I have homework?
names of people and people's titles	President Abraham Lincoln was a good president. Mr. and Mrs. Gonzalez work in the store. Prince William will be the King of England. Professor Hartman is challenging.
places you can find on a map (i.e. countries, states, oceans, cities, etc.).	Newark New York Kean University Pocono Mountains Pacific Ocean Morris Avenue
names of nationalities and languages, religions, ethnic groups	English Muslim Native American Hispanic Catholic Puerto Rican
Days, months and holidays	July Friday Martin Luther King Junior Day

<u>Activity 6</u>

The sentences below have problems with capitalization and with punctuation (. ? !). Correct the sentences.

1. did sarah go to the party
2. the classmates are happy with their teacher
3. my mother works part time
4. what days do you have english class
5. did you visit florida on your vacation
6. the students wrote a paragraph about a family member
7. do you go shopping in new york city

8. is your phone very important to you

9. i have a new computer for school

10. my boyfriend and i go to the movies on friday nights

<u>Activity 7</u>

Correct the paragraphs: add capital letters and periods:

i have a new classmate named maria she is from peru we sit in english class together she has 1 brother and 1 sister they all live in the united states her favorite kind of music is k-pop i think we will be good friends

my new classmate henry is very funny he makes everyone laugh i don't think the teacher likes him henry has curly brown hair and blue eyes he wears nice clothes he listens to music when he does class work he gets good grades i am glad henry is in my class

Activity 8

Build 10 sentences in your notebook using the chart below. Then, underline and label the subjects and double underline the verbs. Do not forget capital letters, periods and question marks.

Subject	Verb	
He	is	a student
My classmate	has	video games
Sarah	goes	soccer
My mother	works	at McDonalds
My friend	likes	to work
	plays	books for school
	studies	to the movies
	buys	cars
		all night
		happy

S V

Ex: My mother works all night.

S V

Ex: He buys cars.

Activity 9

Build 10 sentences in your notebook using the chart below. Then, underline and label the subjects and double underline the verbs. Do not forget capital letters, periods and question marks.

Subject	Verb	
We	are	at a restaurant
My roommates	have	to music
They	like	dogs and cats
The students	listen	in New York City
My sister and I	eat	cake
My parents	work	sad
		every day
		talking on the phone

S V

Ex: My roommates listen to music.

TYPES OF SUBJECTS

1. **Singular Subject**: There is just one subject.

For example:

S
The car is difficult to drive.

S
Diana is a very beautiful girl.

2. **Plural Subject:** More than one person, place or thing.

For example:

S
Children enjoy playing on the playground.

S S
Cynthia and Nora are best friends.

S S
The cat and the dog like to run.

3. **Pronouns as Subjects:** A pronoun (he, she, it, I, you, we, they) can be a subject.

For example:

S
She speaks English very well.

S
We travelled all night by bus.

S
It is raining outside today.

4. **Complete Subject:** This is the actual subject noun plus the words that describe the noun.

For example:

S
The big brown dog eats a lot of food.

S
His beautiful fiancé is very kind.

S
The happy children swam all day at the beach.

TYPES OF VERBS

There are 3 kinds of verbs in English that you need to know:

1. **Active Verb:** There is physical action (walk, run, go, come)

For example:

V
She goes to the university every day.

V
The students study for their final exams.

V
The kids ride their bicycles in the summer.

2. **Non-active Verb**: There is no physical action (have, feel, be--am, are, was, were, think, like)

For example:

V
He is very happy.

V
Children enjoy going to the park.

V
I think about my grades all the time.

3. **Compound Verb:** Some verbs have helping verbs (auxiliary verbs). These verbs give information about the verb tense or they help the verb take on a negative or a question form.

For example: (helping verb is in green, main verb is in red):

Maria is having a party on Friday.

Does he work on weekends?

I have studied English for 1 year.

You do not like exercising.

Jose can cook very well.

4. **Two Verbs:** Sometimes there are 2 different verbs in a sentence.

For example:

V V

We walk around the park and play on the playground every day.

V V V

Babies eat, cry and sleep all day.

V V

The students work on the weekends and study during the week.

Activity 8

Locate and label the subjects and the verbs in these sentences.

S V

Ex: My doctor's appointment is every Monday at 1:10 pm.

1. Charles and Andrew can play basketball really well.
2. I do not have homework tonight.
3. My family and I have lived in the United States for 2 years.
4. The big dog runs to the door and barks at the mailman.
5. We are going to a restaurant for dinner.

6. Kevin and Anne will not drink coffee in the evenings.
7. Teenagers enjoy playing video games.
8. The flowers are sitting on the table.
9. English is difficult to learn.
10. The soccer team is practicing every Monday evening.
11. Rachel read that book and liked it very much.
12. Do you have a car?
13. Jonathan and I went shopping for some clothes for school.
14. The professor did not give us a test.
15. Is your sister coming to your birthday?

Circle the helping verbs in this activity.

Activity 9

Write 10 sentences describing yourself in your notebook. Identify all the subjects and verbs in your sentences.

S V
Ex 1: I am from Cuba.

S V
Ex 2: I play soccer with my friends on the weekend.

www.ingramcontent.com/pod-product-compliance
Lightning Source LLC
LaVergne TN
LVHW060455061126
851857LV00016B/1843
9798385152230